How To Doodle Characters
& Enjoy the Process
An Interactive Guide to Drawing Characters With the Author

Written & Illustrated by
Adriana M Kidd

This book belongs to:

_____

Returning information:

_____

*This book was intended as a character design reference guide for Grade 8+ reading level (13-14 years old) and up

For more artwork by the Author/Illustrator, you can visit:

Facebook: Drawings & Art by Addie Kidd

Or
Instagram: @addiemarieart

Creativity is an art.

NEVER STOP CREATING.

Make your characters come to life.

Table of Contents:

*There are blank pages for you to draw along on to get started all throughout this book!! (& at the very end pg. 41-50)

RECOMMENDED TOOLS TO HAVE ON HAND:

Pencils: Different thicknesses and brands, mechanical pencils work great as well!

Pencil-Sharpener

Pens: All pens are great for sketching– even the ones running out of ink can be used for "light" sketch lines.   Smudging pens are GREAT for drawing movement.

Paint: If desired– Use Watercolors from a tube or pallet. Gouache works great too! Both are "revivable" w/water.

Brush Types: Small, slender and pointed. Make sure they will make the types of swipes needed to color your character.

Ink: India Ink & a thin paint brush works great!

Colored-Pencils: Blue for the line art and red for the solid lines.

    & Any other tools or brands you desire to try or continue using.

*An extra sketchbook if you want to do more than a handful of doodles of each subject mentioned in this book: There are only a handful of blank pages throughout this book and the were meant for "getting you started & thinking about each character design.

About the Author & Book:

I am a self-taught Artist who has always had a love for drawing people and fun characters. This book is a reference of my personal process for sketching character Designs. I wanted to create this "map" to aid you in developing your own characters!

How to Doodle Characters & Enjoy the Process was designed to be a fun guide filled with tips, concept ideas, and sketches for me to share with you in helping you become more enthusiastic about character design!
*This guide was created to help you develop your own style and way of designing <u>Cartoon Characters</u>, so feel free to pick and choose the concepts you value most as guidelines in advancing your character design process. *It also has places for you to sketch in as well!
I am a self-taught Artist who has always had a love for drawing people and fun characters. This book is a reference of my personal process for sketching character Designs. I wanted to create this "map" to aid you in developing your own characters!

Thank you to all my readers for purchasing/receiving this sketch guide to character design! I hope you will enjoy following along this unique and open design process.

–Addie

Intro to the Character Design Process

First, you will need to consider the type of character you want to create. Are they BOLD and BRAVE or shy and mild...? Establish the overall FEEL of how your character would "light up a room". Is their presence menacing and dangerous? Are they attractive and elegant?

You decide!

When you draw, consider the line-weight: Is the texture of the pencil/pen you are using not giving your character the right look...? Consider using a different approach, use a different size, or choose another tool altogether.

Different pens and pencils create different line-weights as well as different pencils. Experiment often!

"Bird Lady" 2019 by Addie Kidd

How to draw those "swooshy-flowy-lines"

This technique takes time and practice to achieve without making a poorly-drawn *swoosh*... Everyone says it but yes– practice! Even if that means re-drawing that same line over and over again... Your determination and persistence will pay off. If you make a mistake with pen– get creative and disguise it as something else! Art requires creativity in all the stages, and sometimes, especially in mistakes. Turn that accidental smudge into another strand of hair... Make that random dot part of the outfit. If it does not work out: re-draw it! It's okay– there are some unfixable mistakes and they become learning curves.

The Smudging Approach:

A combination of the *swooshy-line art*, and smearing ink/graphite on paper for "movement" and/or "depth" texture. This is great for concept sketches especially. If you want to portray movement without just fine lines going in one direction, try smearing the lines to add some shading and character to your character.
A concept sketch doesn't have to be detailed, but it should be recognizable and distinct.

"Warrior" by Addie Kidd

Practice Page

Practice Page

Eyes

If you're *looking* for your character to have emotion, you can find it in the *eyes*... This is the element that makes them come to life... Show their "living" *soul* in the eyes. Eyes can capture a lot of emotion alone: fear, sadness, love, being tired, *etc. For good character design with eyes, unique features is key.

For sad eyes: Make the lines shaped like curves of a tear drop, droopy at the corners, rounded on the top and bottom. Add lots of glistening reflective dots in the eyes as well!

For happy eyes: All the lines are excited!- Make even the eyelashes "swoop" for joy... Try using bright and warm colors to give it a

Practice Page

Practice Page

Expressions

Expressions can be extremely exaggerated with cartoon-y cartoon character designs. Try drawing some super "stretched" or "squashed" facial expressions! Emotion is important… What is going through the character's mind? How are they feeling in the situation you're putting them in? Disturbed? Scared? Happy? Try creating some unusual and unique expressions!

Besides body poses, expression is the next best way to capture how the character is *feeling*. Even the lightest change in eyebrow shape can alter the way the character's expression is drawn. If you want to get better at drawing a full facial expression that ties in the whole face, make sure to have all the lines arranged "harmoniously"... (see below) This character's expression consists of raised eyebrows, one with a slight curve, and a lot of rounded curved lines: this gives the expression a "wide" look. Practice drawing expressions on the next few pages! Expressions are fun when exaggerated as well.

*Make sure that the eyes, eyebrows, nose, and mouth all look "harmonious".

"Sea Monster"   "Looking Left" By Addie Kidd

Practice Page

Practice Page

Poses

The image below is pose mixed with expression, mixed with movement... the body is shaped sort of like an "S": a cartoon-y stance of swaying and being "cute". Try coming up with neat shapes for the character's overall body to be shaped and go from there... Blocky and square, thin and tall, curved and rounded, experiment! But make sure it's balanced, and if it's off-set like the image below, make the weight distributed evenly so it looks exaggerated but convincing.

Direction is important with poses and action drawing! How is the artwork guiding your eye across the page? Is everything coming together or pulling apart…? Is there a pattern or a visual rhythm? Are the lines the same or are there numerous line-weights used throughout the character? Do they look messy or clean and is this aligning with who they are supposed to be as you intended? Everything contributes to how your character looks when it comes to designing a sound character. Make sure you pay attention to these things, and soon enough, they will become second nature.

Poses: continued...

Make the movement flow together so everything looks connected. Use harmony. In the image below, look at how the weight of the body is being shifted backwards from tugging on the rope. Practice drawing "force" movements showing something being heavy in the arms of your character as they struggle to lift it. Or come up with your own scenario on the next few pages!

Practice Page

Practice Page

Female-Focused Design

Female facial shapes tend to be rounder than men's, and in cartoons– the eyes are more "feminine" with exaggerated lashes and small-er, dainty noses. Women have curves in their leg shape and hips, with smaller feet and hands.

Practice Page

Practice Page

Male-Focused Design

Men's facial shapes are primarily longer/ more
square (chiseled) than female facial shapes.
Noses tend to be longer, and eyebrows bushier.
Men have rounded shoulders and wide torso,
with big hands and feet.

Practice Page

Practice Page

Extra References for Inspiration...

Use guide-lines to form the facial shape and angle. This concept was drawn with pen: does not smudge like graphite. Clean line strokes and consistent line weight control. Remember to sketch lightly with pen if you are not absolutely sure/confident about the lines you are putting down. Think of it as sculpting or chiseling away and forming a face out of a white space. Take your time, speed comes with practice and experience with your tools.

Drawing big "puffy" lines will give the texture of floating fabric, which works great for clothing designs. Ball-gowns especially. Curved lines work well for wavy hair, too. Make sure they all "flow" together and all the lines look like they complete the image and not take away from the design itself.

Try mixed-media! This piece was created with India Ink and black Watercolors after being sketched out first. Different mediums will give you different textures, as well as different tools used to distribute your substances. Get creative! Make artwork with dark and light colors, tones, and detailing. Don't forget to experiment with backgrounds too!

I hope you had fun and enjoyed going through this book on helping you get started designing your own characters!

Remember to draw often, there will always be something new to learn!

Try new tactics and approaches as much as possible to find unique ways to make your Character Design stand out!

*There is more space for you to doodle/ and design with on the next handful of pages!............

Thank you for reading!
-Addie

Practice Page

Practice Page

Practice Page

Practice Page

Practice Page

Practice Page

Practice Page

Practice Page

Practice Page

Practice Page

www.ingramcontent.com/pod-product-compliance
Lightning Source LLC
Chambersburg PA
CBHW061222280526
45784CB00006B/2593